WILMA P. MANKILLER
Chief of the Cherokee

WILMA P. MANKILLER
Chief of the Cherokee

By Charnan Simon

CHILDRENS PRESS ®
CHICAGO

Dedication
To my daughters Ariel and Hana

Photo Credits

AP/ Wide World Photo: 11
© Gwendolen Cates: cover, 1, 3
Stuart Bratesman/Dartmouth College: 31
© Emilie Lepthien: 6, 7, 8, 16, 20, 21 (2 photos)
Cherokee Nation of Oklahoma: 5, 12, 15, 23, 25, 26, 27, 30; © Dan
 Agent, 29
Photri / © Mark Myers: 14, 17, 19, 22
UPI / Bettmann Newsphotos: 28

Project editor: E. Russell Primm III
Design and electronic composition: Biner Design
Photo research: Judith Feldman

The editors wish to thank the Cherokee Nation for its kind support
and cooperation during the development of this biography. Dan
Agent and his co-workers were unfailingly patient.

Library of Congress Cataloging-in-Publication Data

Simon, Charnan.
    Wilma Mankiller : chief of the Cherokee / by Charnan Simon.
    p. cm. — (Picture story biography)
    Summary: Describes the life of the Indian activist who became the first woman Principal
Chief of the Cherokee Nation.
    ISBN 0-516-04181-9
    1. Mankiller, Wilma P., 1945- — Juvenile literature. 2. Cherokee Indians —
Biography — Juvenile literature. 3. Cherokee Indians — Social conditions — Juvenile
literature. [1. Mankiller, Wilma P., 1945- . 2. Cherokee Indians — Biography. 3. Indians
of North America—Biography.] I. Title. II. Series: Picture- story biographies.

E99.C5M337 1991   91-4334
973'.04975—dc20   CIP
[B]   AC

In the old days, the Cherokees called it "having a good mind." A person with a good mind thinks positively about both people and happenings. When hard times come, she doesn't give up. She takes what has been done and turns it into a better path. Wilma Mankiller's Cherokee ancestors would be proud of her. She has a good mind.

Wilma Pearl Mankiller was born at the Indian hospital in Tahlequah, Oklahoma, on November 18, 1945. Her father, Charlie, was a full-blooded Cherokee Indian. Her mother, Irene, was of Dutch-Irish descent. Wilma and her six brothers and four sisters grew up on a farm. Their house had no plumbing and no electricity, but the children were happy – and busy!

Before the government moved Wilma, her parents, and her ten brothers and sisters to San Francisco, the Mankiller family lived on a farm and worked the land.

Wilma has fond memories of working in her family's strawberry garden. This photo shows an example of a Cherokee farm.

They rode horseback to the nearby spring for clear, cool water. They weeded the strawberry patch and fed the animals. During the day, the sun shone brightly in the blue prairie sky. At night, a million stars twinkled overhead. Wilma liked life on the wide open prairie.

Then, in 1957, everything changed. For two years, no rain fell. The land dried up, and the strawberries died.

The family could no longer earn a living on their farm. They would have to move.

The government said it would help. The Bureau of Indian Affairs moved Charlie Mankiller and his family to San Francisco. The Bureau moved many Indian families off their farms and into cities during the 1950s. This relocation was supposed to give the Indians more jobs and better houses.

The Bureau of Indian Affairs in Washington, D.C., decided to move many rural Indians from their homes into large cities during the 1950s.

It was called "mainstreaming." It took Indians out of the country and dropped them smack in the middle of mainstream America.

Moving to San Francisco was like landing on another planet for twelve-year-old Wilma and her brothers and sisters. The noise, the traffic, the crowded buildings – they had never seen anything like it. When they heard sirens blaring on their first night, they dived under the covers in terror. They wanted to go home to the prairie!

In many ways, life was harder in the city than it had been on the farm. The government had moved the Mankillers to a rough part of San Francisco. Charlie and Irene worked hard to provide for their children, but the family was still poor. Wilma's oldest brother had to drop out of school to earn money. Worst of all was the loneliness. In Oklahoma, they had been surrounded by Cherokee friends and neighbors. In San Francisco, they were alone.

Eventually, Wilma got used to city living. She went to school and rode a bicycle and talked on the telephone like millions of other American girls. After high school, she attended classes at San Francisco State University. It was there that she met and married a businessman from the South American country of Ecuador. With him, she traveled to South America and Europe. Back in San Francisco, Wilma soon settled into life as a wife and mother to two daughters, Felicia, born in 1964, and Gina, born in 1966.

Then, in 1969, Wilma Mankiller's life changed again. Wilma heard about some Indian students who didn't like the way their people were being treated by the rest of America. These students staged a protest to draw attention to the Indians' problems. They took over the former federal prison on Alcatraz Island. They vowed to stay until something was done to help their people.

Wilma was very impressed by these students. She realized that she, too, was angry and upset about the mistreatment of her Indian brothers and sisters. As the

The Indian occupation of Alcatraz Island in 1970 was the beginning of Wilma Mankiller's interest in Indian rights.

Wilma Mankiller presents Johnny Backwater with a certificate honoring his work on a self-help housing project in Kenwood, Oklahoma. Wilma's interest in Indians working to better themselves began in San Francisco when Alcatraz Island was taken over.

mother of two young daughters, Wilma couldn't camp out with the protesters on, Alcatraz. But she could tell people about them and raise money to help them.

And so Wilma Mankiller became an activist for Indian rights. First, she did fund-raising for the protesters on

Alcatraz. Then she went back to school to learn more about sociology and community development. She got a job as Native American Programs Coordinator with the Oakland Public Schools. Her life was very busy.

Wilma was busy, but she was not completely happy. Her marriage was not working out very well. Years of city life had made her tired. She was worried about Felicia and Gina, too. She wanted her daughters to know the kind of country life she had enjoyed as a child.

So, in 1976, Wilma took her daughters and moved home to Oklahoma. Her father, who had died in 1971, was buried there, and her mother had moved back to be near friends and family. One by one, Wilma and her brothers and sisters began moving home, too.

At first, Wilma was busy enough just settling her two daughters into their new life. After the hectic pace of San Francisco, she was happy to slow down a little bit.

It wasn't long, however, before Wilma began turning her energies outwards. She and her family had settled in Adair County, just east of the town of Tahlequah. And Tahlequah was the headquarters of the Cherokee Nation of Oklahoma. Before long, Wilma was volunteering her time and talents to help her people in the Cherokee Nation.

The seal of the Cherokee Nation

Ambassador Julie Zvobago of Zimbabwe visited Tahlequah, Oklahoma, in 1987 as part of a thirty-day tour of the United States. Ambassador Zvobago was shown the Cherokee Nation's work on youth and women's issues.

Wilma started out by writing grant applications to get federal funds for various tribal programs. But Wilma didn't want the Cherokees to depend on the United States government for help. She wanted them to be independent. She remembered what had happened to her family when they let the government move them to San Francisco from their family home in Oklahoma. Wilma was convinced that only the Cherokees themselves knew best how to solve Cherokee problems.

After all, they had done so many times in the past. When Europeans first settled in America, the Cherokees were a proud and thriving nation – the largest of what came to be known as the Five Civilized Tribes. Spread out all over the Southeast, the Cherokees were generous and helpful to their new white neighbors.

When Europeans first encountered the Cherokees, they lived in houses made of woven river cane plastered with river clay such as this one.

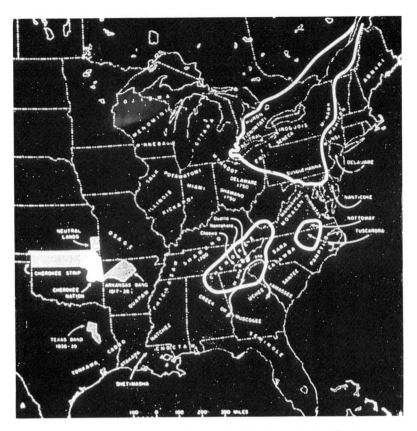

This map shows the Indian tribes in the Eastern United States,
including the Cherokee, during the early 1800s.

Unfortunately, their white neighbors
were not very generous to them. In
1838, President Andrew Jackson
pushed the Cherokees out of their
homes in Georgia, Tennessee, and the
Carolinas. The lands they had lived on
for years would now belong to white
families instead of Cherokee families.

First President Jackson robbed the Cherokees of millions of acres of land. Then he forced them to march 1,200 miles to the newly created Indian Territory in northeastern Oklahoma. Some 16,000 Cherokees made this march. More than 4,000 of them, men, women, and children, died before they ever reached Oklahoma. Forever after, Cherokees would mourn this as a true "Trail of Tears."

They would mourn, but they would not give up. Pushed to the edge of the American frontier, the Cherokees turned their energies to taming this new land. They drew up a constitution, built roads and schools, and settled farms and ranches. Their thriving community was the envy of their white neighbors.

Then came the Civil War. Some Cherokees sided with the North. Some

This famous painting shows the Cherokee people's journey to the west, often called "The Trail of Tears."

sided with the South. Like the rest of the United States, the Cherokee Nation was torn apart by this horrible war.

After the war, more and more white Americans moved west. They crowded out the Cherokees and other Indians. In 1907, the Indian Territory that had been promised to the Cherokees was taken from them and made into the state of Oklahoma. The Cherokee Nation was no more.

It wasn't until 1946 that the United States government allowed the Cherokee Nation to reorganize. Slowly,

The Cherokee Supreme Court building in New Echota, Georgia

the nation set to work. It developed jobs and industries for Cherokees to work at. It set up health services and job training centers. It built Cherokee schools and began teaching the old Cherokee ways of life. But all the time,

One of Chief Mankiller's interests is keeping alive the traditional Cherokee way of life, including the language, arts, and crafts. At left, a woman weaves a basket, and, below, an example of a dug-out canoe.

the nation's chief was appointed by the president of the United States. It wasn't until 1971 that the Cherokees were allowed to elect their own chief. Once again, Cherokees were taking control of their own lives.

The Cherokee Chiefs from 1828–1916

Wilma Mankiller has continually worked for adequate housing for all Cherokees. Here, Chief Mankiller presents a check to the director of Oaks Indian Mission, a home for abused and abandoned children.

And that was the way Wilma Mankiller wanted to keep it when she went home to Oklahoma in 1976. She saw that two of the things rural Cherokees needed most were better homes and running water. So she began teaching some people how to build and repair their own houses. Using materials provided by the tribe, she helped others install their own water systems.

Chief Ross Swimmer soon noticed this bright, dedicated organizer. He encouraged all her hard work. By 1979, Wilma was tribal planner and program development specialist for the Cherokee Nation. She was also taking graduate classes at the nearby University of Arkansas.

Then, in 1979, tragedy struck. Wilma was driving home from classes on November 9. A car coming from the other direction was trying to pass. It ran directly into Wilma Mankiller's station wagon.

Wilma was in the hospital for months. Her legs were shattered, her ribs were broken, and her face was smashed. At first, doctors thought she would never walk again. But seventeen operations saved her legs, and plastic surgery restored her face.

Wilma still didn't feel right, however. She stumbled a lot and kept dropping things. That's when she found out she had myasthenia gravis, a serious disease that affects the nervous system. It was back to the hospital for Wilma, for more surgery and a long program of chemotherapy.

By 1981, Wilma was back on the job. She continued to help the rural Cherokees of Oklahoma help themselves. In 1983, Chief Ross Swimmer asked her to run as his Deputy Chief. Together, they won the

Wilma was inducted into the Oklahoma Hall of Fame in 1986. She is shown here with Lucille Hurd-Hitson and Grace Hudlin, two other inductees.

Wilma Mankiller is sworn in as Principal Chief of the Cherokee Nation after Chief Swimmer became Director of the Bureau of Indian Affairs in 1985.

election. Then, in 1985, Chief Swimmer went to Washington, D.C., to become director of the Bureau of Indian Affairs. That left Wilma Mankiller as the first woman Principal Chief of the Cherokee Nation.

Some people didn't think a woman should be chief. But before Europeans came to America, Cherokee women shared tribal power with men. Children belonged to their mother's clan, not their father's. And clan mothers made decisions right along with the men. So when Wilma Mankiller was elected Principal Chief in her own right in 1987, she was taking a step forward and a step backward at the same time. When she was reelected chief in 1991, no one doubted that Wilma Mankiller could do the job.

Today, Chief Mankiller is busier than ever. As head of the Cherokee Nation, she governs 120,000 people

In her position as Chief of the Cherokee Nation, Wilma Mankiller meets with leaders from the United States and from foreign countries. Here, she meets with U.S. Senator Daniel Inouye.

throughout the United States and manages a $55 million annual budget. Being chief of this nation is like being president of a small country.

There are a lot of problems. Many Cherokees are poor and have no jobs. Their houses lack heat and plumbing and electricity, and their roofs leak. But Chief Mankiller has faith in her people. She knows their proud history. She sees their strength and beauty and intelligence.

In her upbeat, determined way, Chief Mankiller is bringing healthy Cherokee communities back to life. She wants

In 1988, Chief Mankiller met with President Ronald Reagan at the White House.

Wilma celebrates the 37th Cherokee National Holiday with her daughter Gina Olaya and grandson Kellen during the Labor Day weekend, 1989.

everyone to have a decent place to live and work and go to school. She wants her people to learn their Cherokee language and culture, and to believe that they can thrive as Indians in today's America. She doesn't want any Cherokee child to go through what she did as a girl.

Wilma Mankiller laughs when you ask about her name. Two hundred years ago, "Mankiller" was a high Cherokee military rank, like a general in the army. One of her ancestors liked the title so much, he took it as his name. Now Chief Mankiller has a high rank, too. Her battle is against poverty and discrimination and discouragement.

Chief Mankiller isn't anything like the Indian chiefs shown in cartoons. She is a wife and a mother and a grandmother. Her husband, Charlie Soap, whom she married in 1986, is a full-blooded Cherokee. He is fluent in

Wilma accepted the Oklahoma Heritage Award from Sanders Mitchell (right) in 1991. Charlie Soap, Chief Mankiller's husband, is in the center.

Chief Wilma Mankiller received an honorary doctoral degree from Dartmouth College for her contributions to the Cherokee people.

the Cherokee language and is teaching Wilma to be, too.

Most of all, Chief Mankiller is a true leader of her people. When asked, she will say, "I want to be remembered as the person who helped us restore faith in ourselves." Like her Cherokee ancestors before her, Chief Wilma Mankiller has a good mind.

WILMA P. MANKILLER

1945   Born November 18, 1945, Tahlequah, Oklahoma

1957   Moved to San Francisco, California, as part of the Bureau of Indian Affairs Relocation Program

1964   Daughter Felicia born

1966   Daughter Gina born

1969   Native American protest on Alcatraz Island marks beginning of her political activism

1975   Moved back to Adair Country, Oklahoma

1977   Economic Stimulus Coordinator, Cherokee Nation of Oklahoma

1979   Bachelor of Science in Social Work, Graduate Work in Commmunity Planning, University of Arkansas; Program Development Specialist, Cherokee Nation of Oklahoma

1981   Director, Cherokee Nation Community Development Department

1983   Elected Deputy Principal Chief, Cherokee Nation of Oklahoma

1985   Appointed Principal Chief, Cherokee Nation of Oklahoma

1986   American Indian Woman of the Year, Oklahoma Federation of Indian Women; married Charlie Soap

1987   Elected Principal Chief, Cherokee Nation of Oklahoma; Woman of the Year, Ms. Magazine

1991   Honorary Doctorate of Humane Letters, Dartmouth University; reelected Principal Chief, Cherokee Nation of Oklahoma

INDEX

ABOUT THE AUTHOR

Charnan Simon grew up in Ohio, Georgia, Oregon, and Washington State. She holds a B.A. degree in English Literature from Carleton College in Northfield, Minnesota, and an M.A. in English Literature from the University of Chicago. She worked for children's trade book companies after college and became the managing editor of Cricket magazine before beginning her career as a free-lance writer. Ms. Simon has written dozens of books and articles for young people and especially likes writing — and reading — history, biography, and fiction of all sorts. She lives in Chicago with her husband and two daughters.